Dear Parent,

Thank you for selecting our letter tracing workbook for your child's learning journey!

This book is designed for children aged 3 to 5, that said older kids can benefit from letter writing practice also. The book helps develop the skills they need to recognize and write letters. It is good to develop fine motor skills and early literacy at this time in your child's life. This workbook is a fun, engaging way for your child to practice tracing and writing letters.

Each page offers plenty of space for practice, encouraging repetition and building confidence as your child progresses. The mix of Letter Tracing, Coloring In and Alphabet Mazes adds variety and fun to the learning process. By completing this workbook, it will help you child not only improve their handwriting skills but also develop the focus and patience needed for more advanced learning in the future.

We hope this Letter Tracing Workbook is enjoyable for both you and your child.

MIND
MOTIVATION
BOOKS

We are a small independent publisher. We have a passion for creating educational and learning pages like these.

Please consider leaving us a review on Amazon. It only takes a few seconds to scan the code below and leave a review. It really helps small publishers like us. We greatly appreciate your support.

SCAN ME

Thank you.

MIND
MOTIVATION
BOOKS

Letter Tracing
for Kids

This Book Belongs to

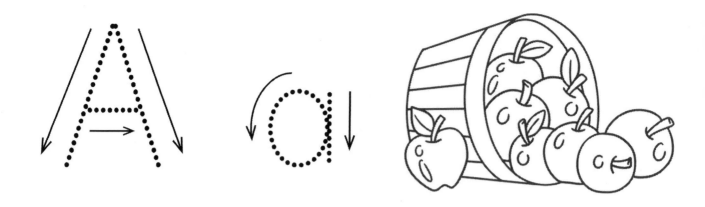

A is for Apple. Color me in

A is for Apple

A A A A A A A A A A A

A A A A A A A A A A A

A A A A A A A A A A A

a a a a a a a a a a a a a

a a a a a a a a a a a a a

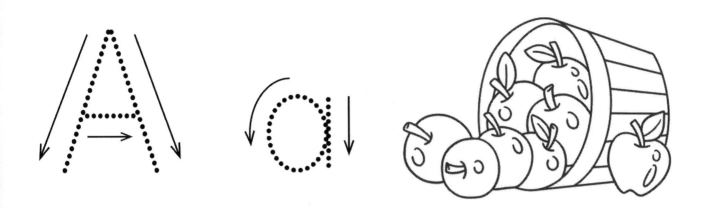

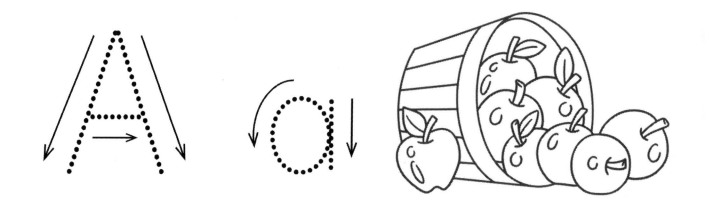

A a A a A a A a A a A a A a

A

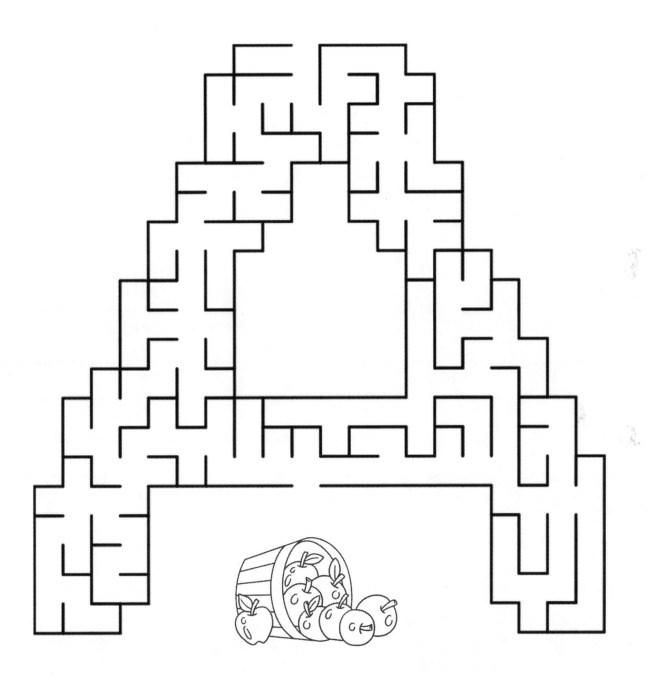

Can you help A find the Apples?

B b

B is for Bird. Color me in

B is for Bird

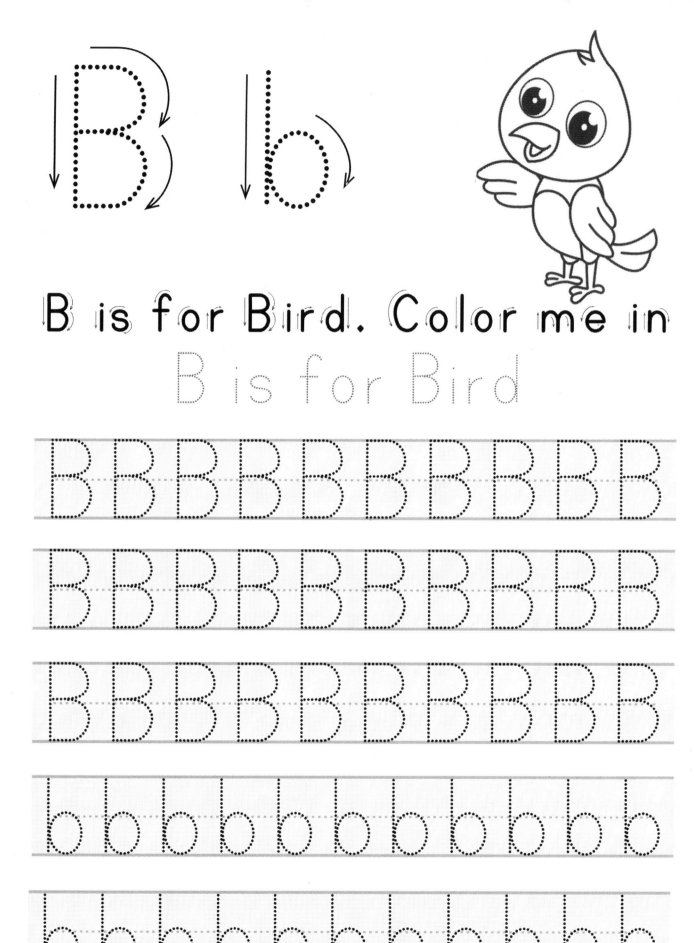

B

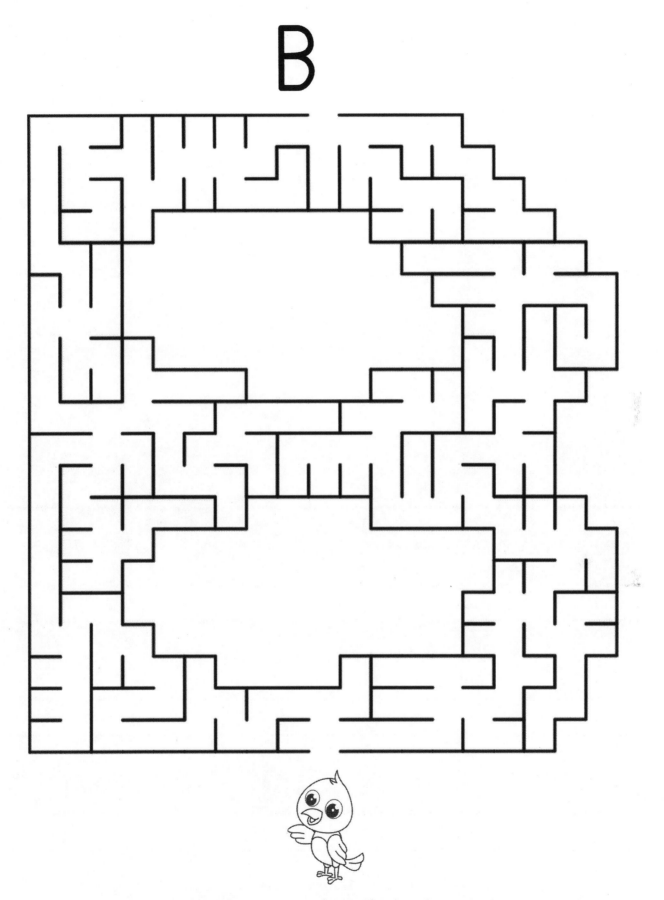

Can you help the Bird find the B ?

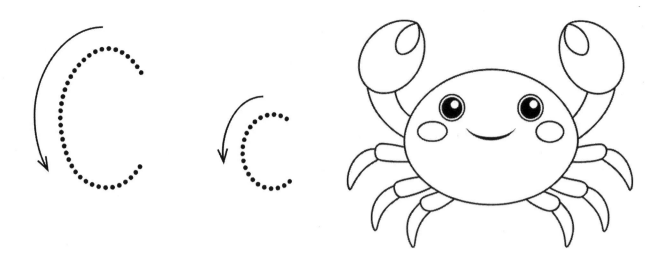

C is for Crab. Color me in

C is for Crab

C C C C C C C C C

C C C C C C C C C

C C C C C C C C C

c c c c c c c c c c c c c

c c c c c c c c c c c c c

C

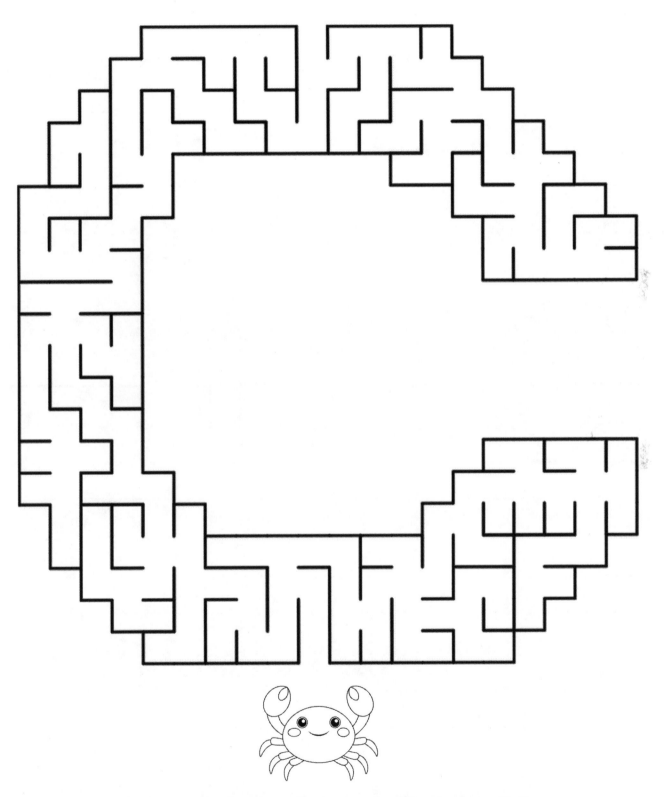

Can you help the Crab find the C ?

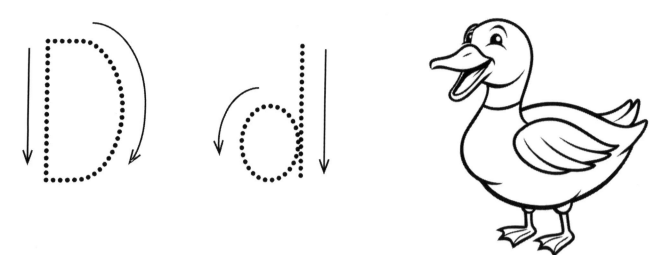

D is for Duck. Color me in

D is for Duck

D D D D D D D D D

D D D D D D D D D

D D D D D D D D D

d d d d d d d d d d d

d d d d d d d d d d d

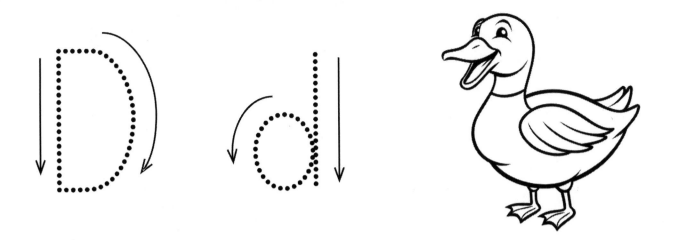

D

Can you help the Duck find the D ?

E is for Elephant. Color me in.

E is for Elephant

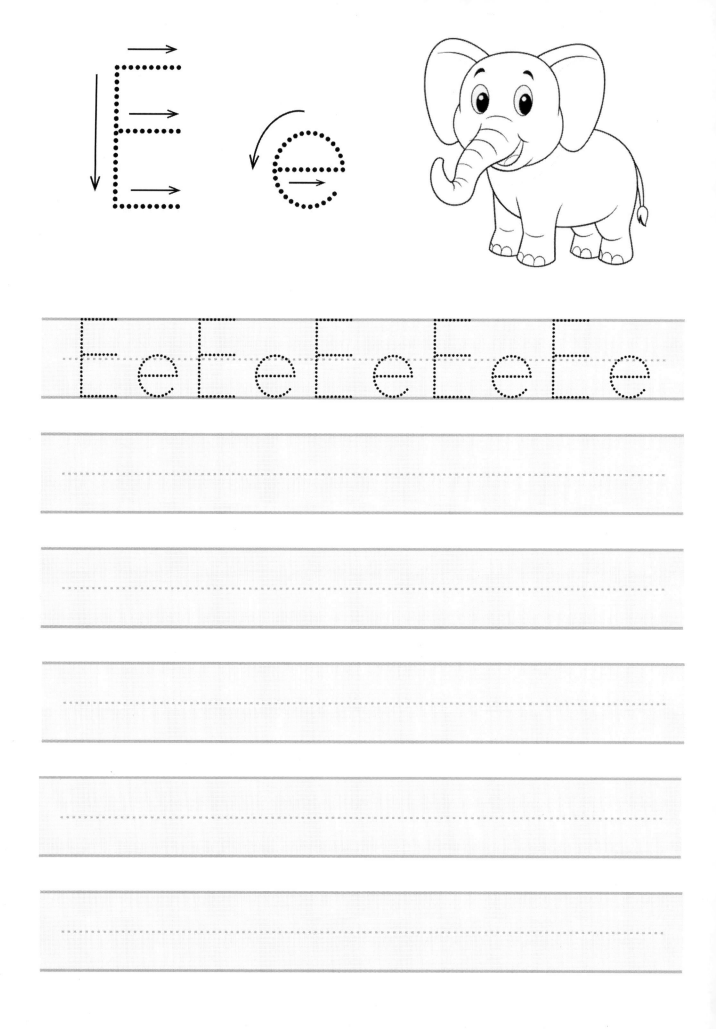

E

Can you help the Elephant find the E ?

F is for Fish. Color me in

F is for Fish

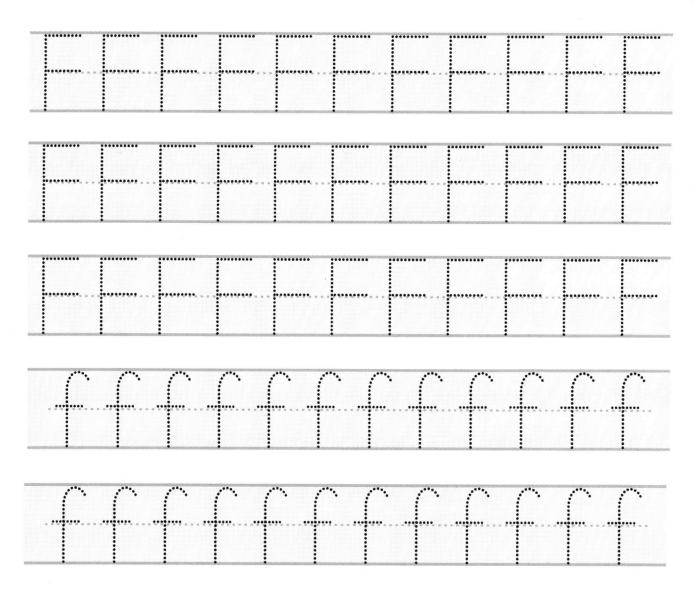

F

Can you help the Fish find the F ?

G is for Giraffe. Color me in.

G is for Giraffe

G G G G G G G G

G G G G G G G G

G G G G G G G G

g g g g g g g g g g

g g g g g g g g g g

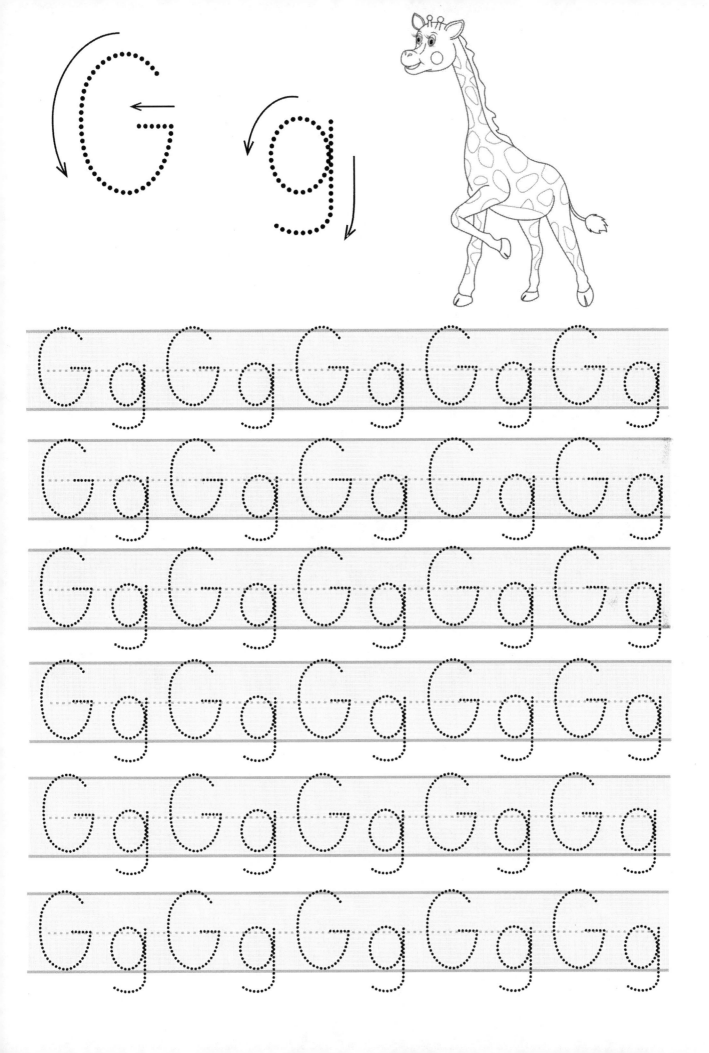

G

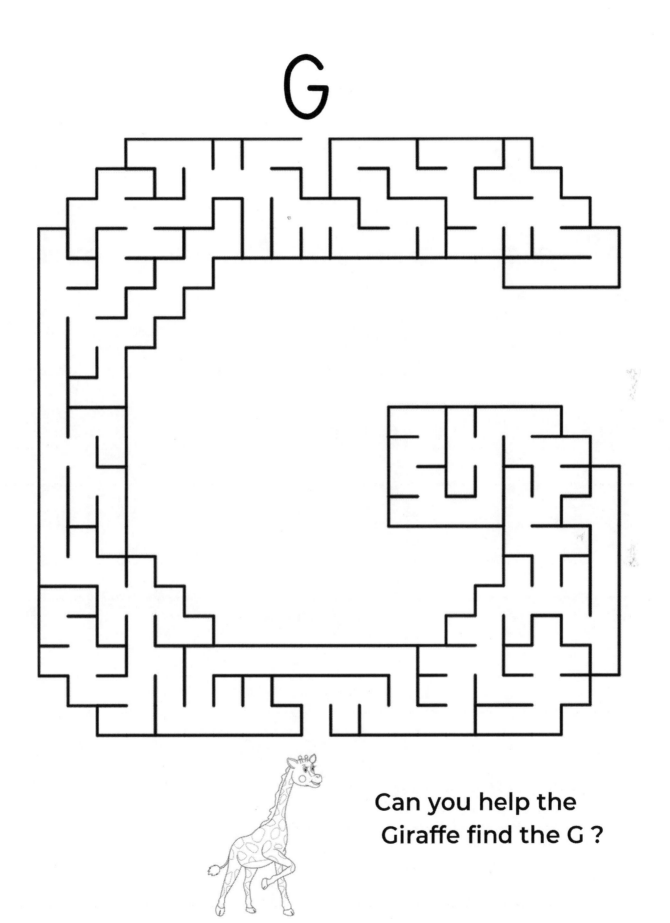

Can you help the
Giraffe find the G ?

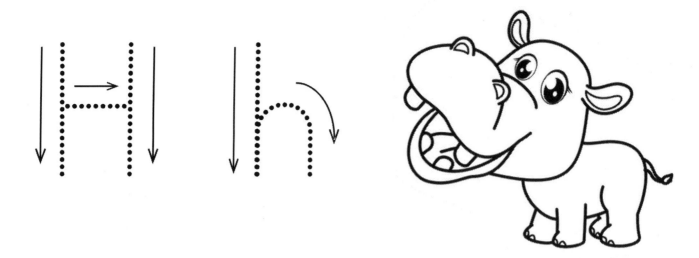

H is for Hippo. Color me in

H is for Hippo

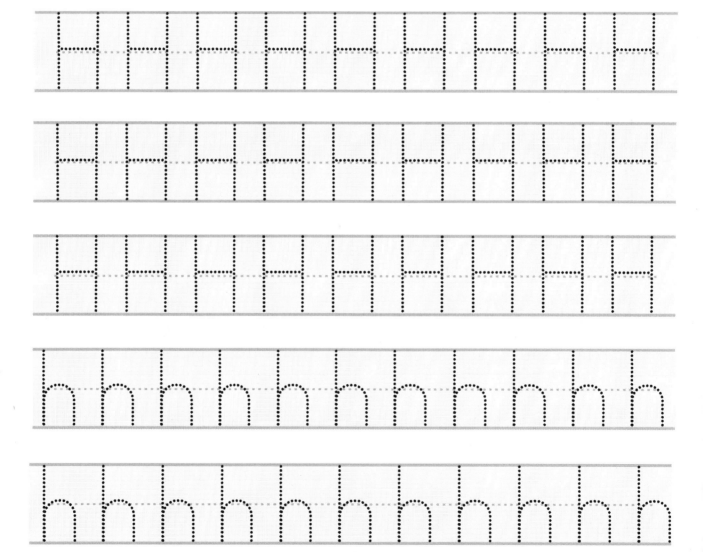

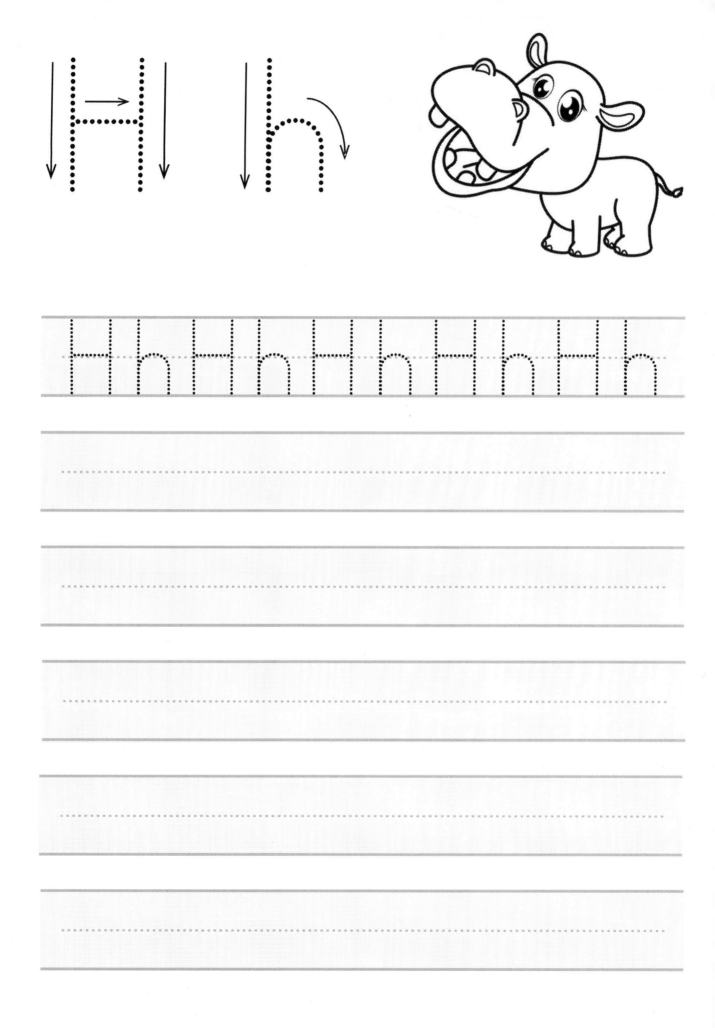

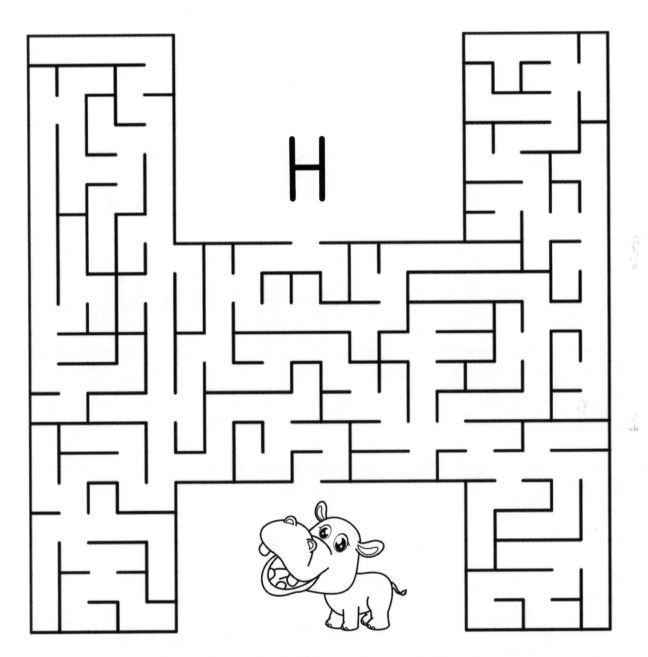

Can you help the Hippo find the H ?

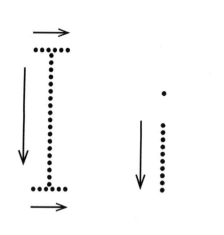 

I is for Icecream. Color me in

I is for Icecream

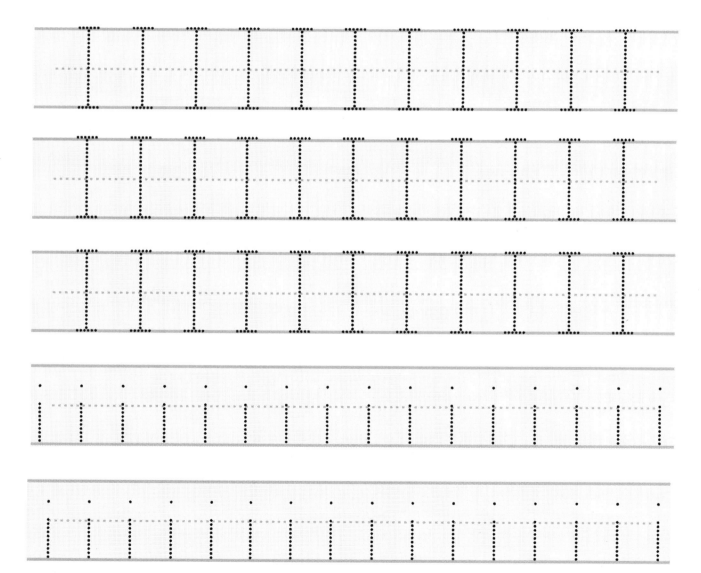

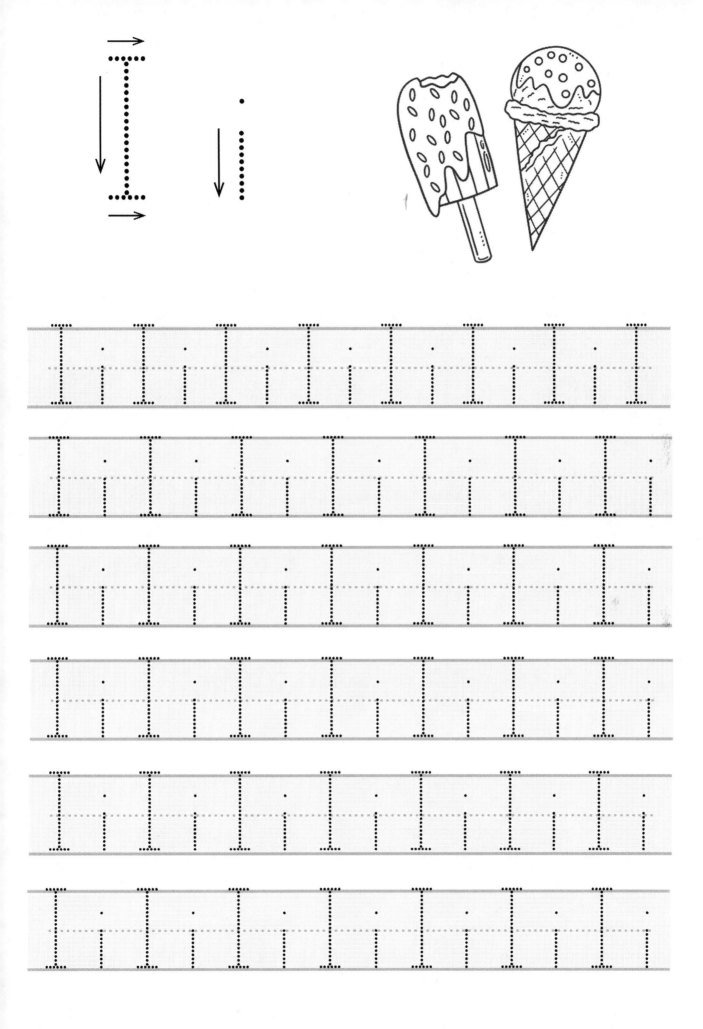

I

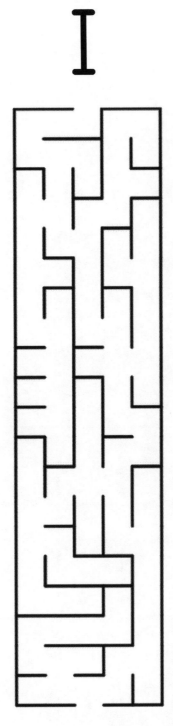

Can you help I
find the Icecream?

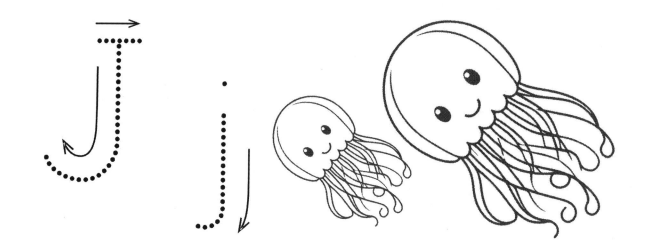

J is for Jellyfish. Color me in

J is for Jellyfish

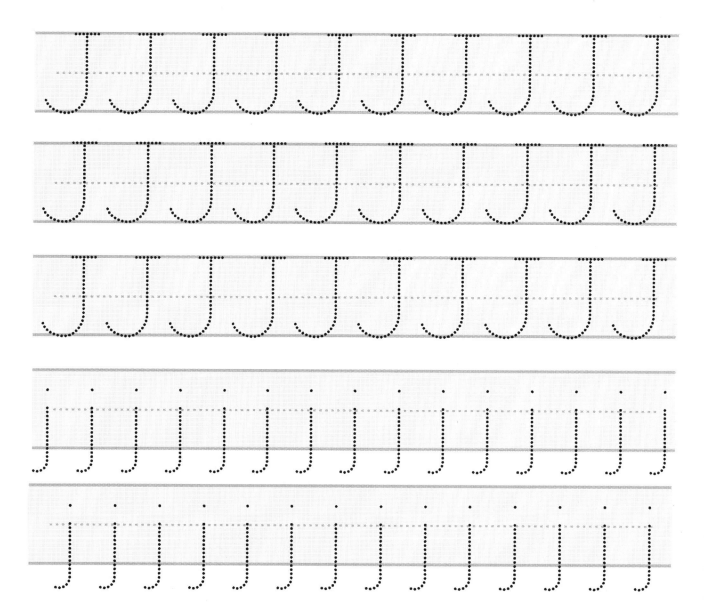

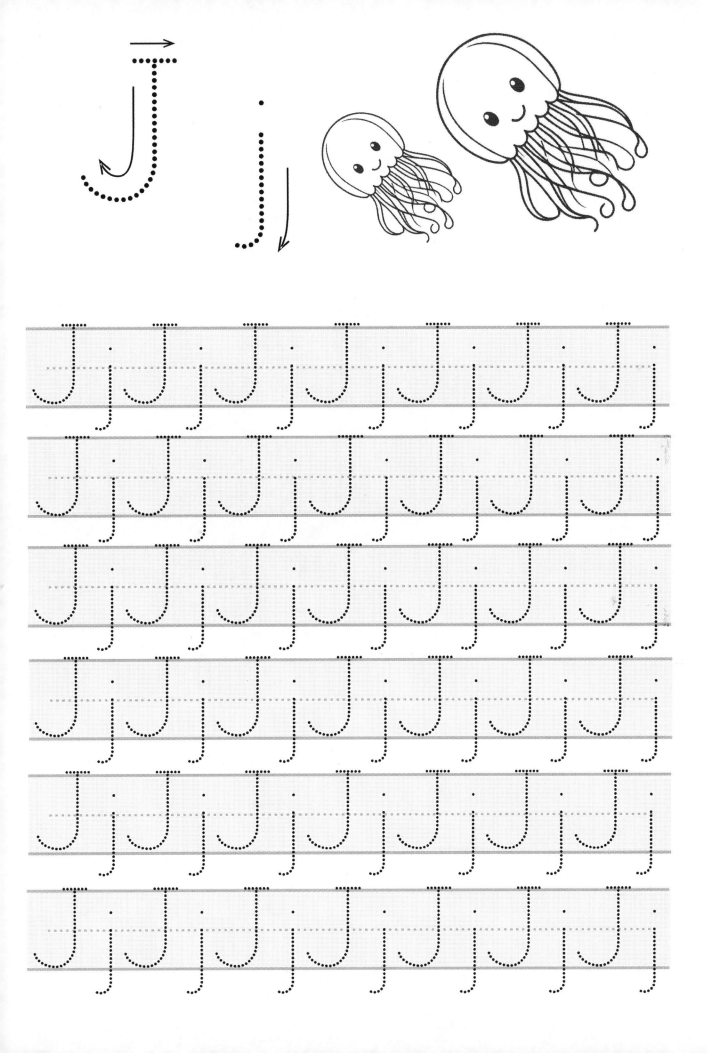

J

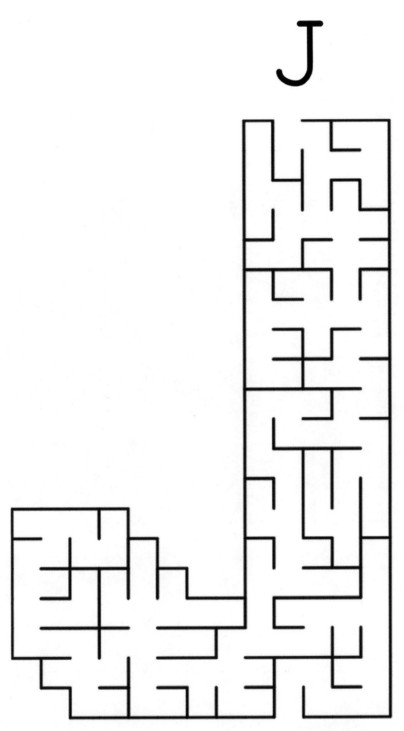

Can you help the
Jellyfish find the J ?

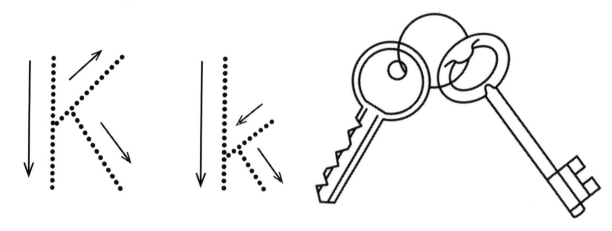

K is for Keys. Color me in

K is for Keys

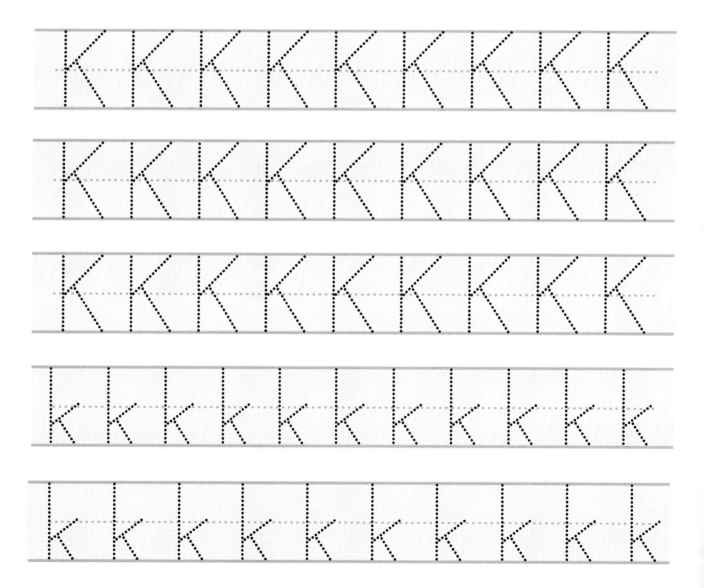

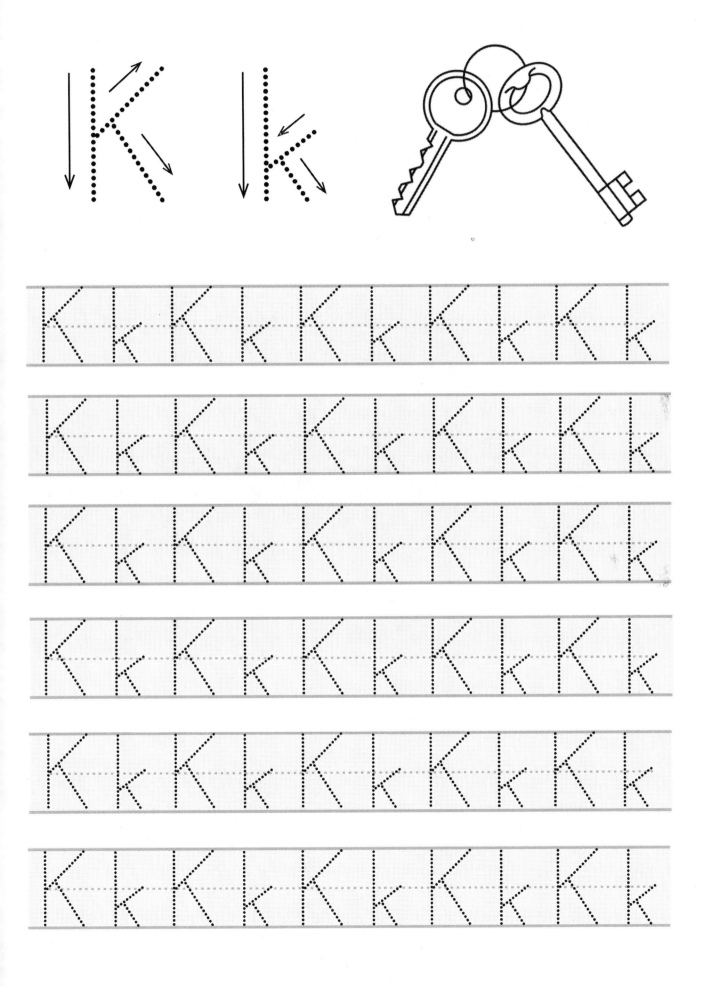

**Can you help K
find the keys ?**

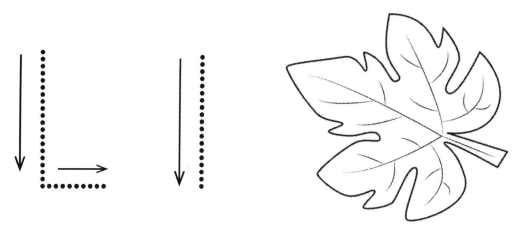

L is for Leaf. Color me in

L is for Leaf

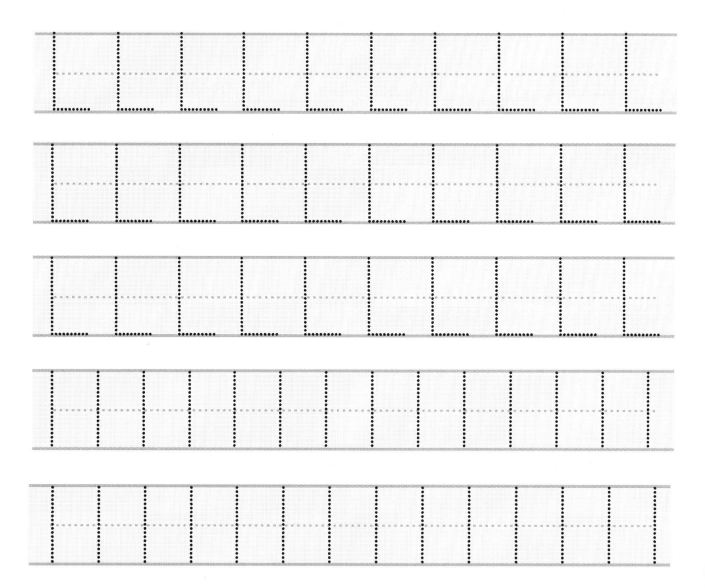

L

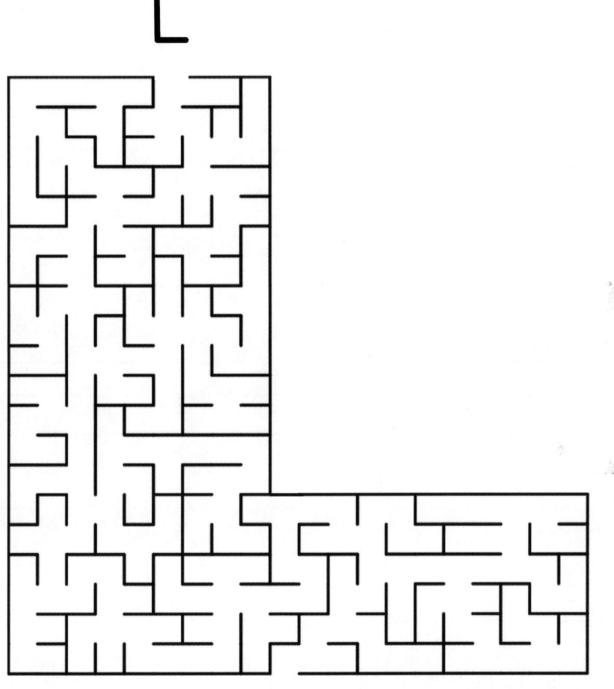

Can you help L
find the Leaf ?

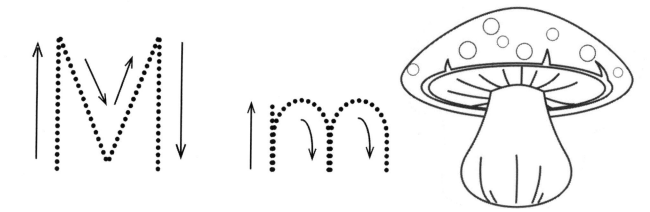

M is for Mushroom . Color me in

M is for Mushroom

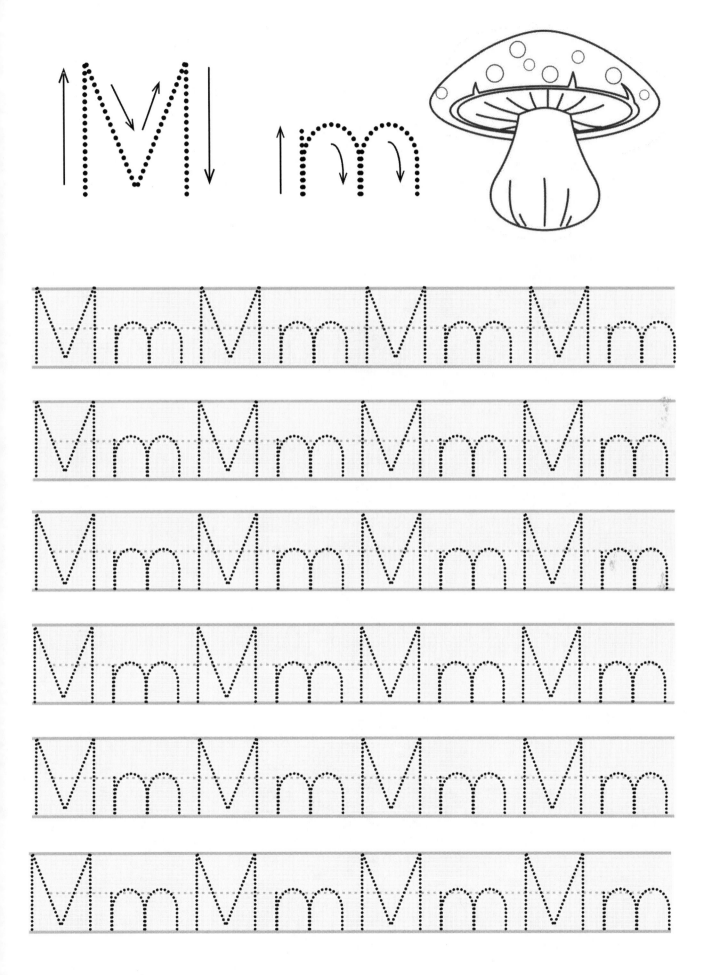

M

Can you help M find the Mushroom ?

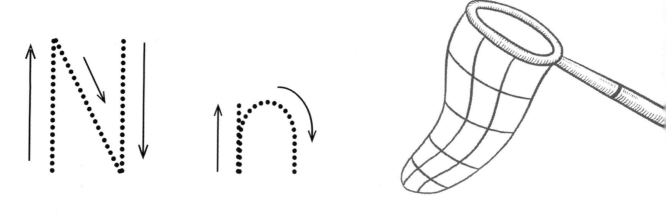

N is for Net. Color me in
N is for Net

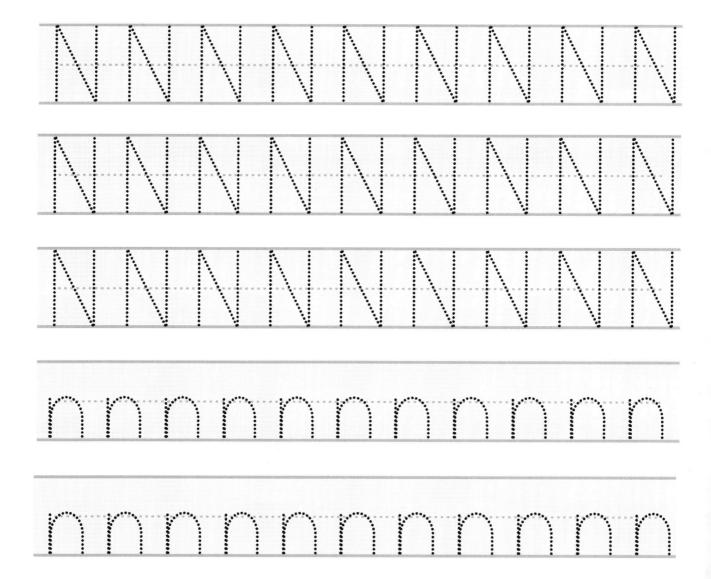

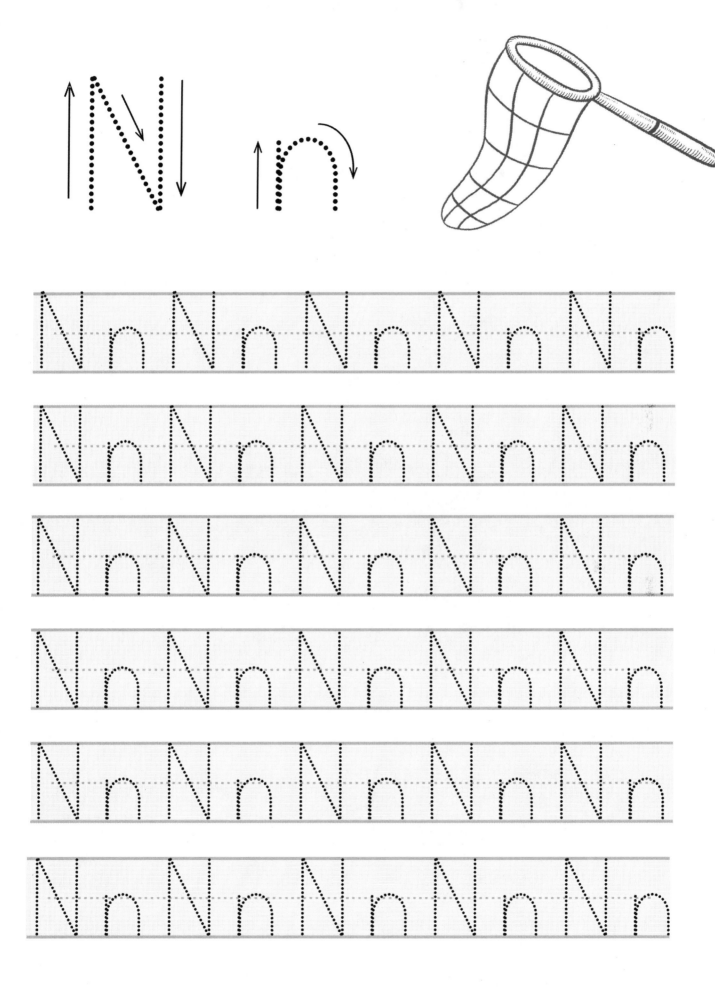

Can you help N
find the Net ?

O is for Owl. Color me in

O is for Owl

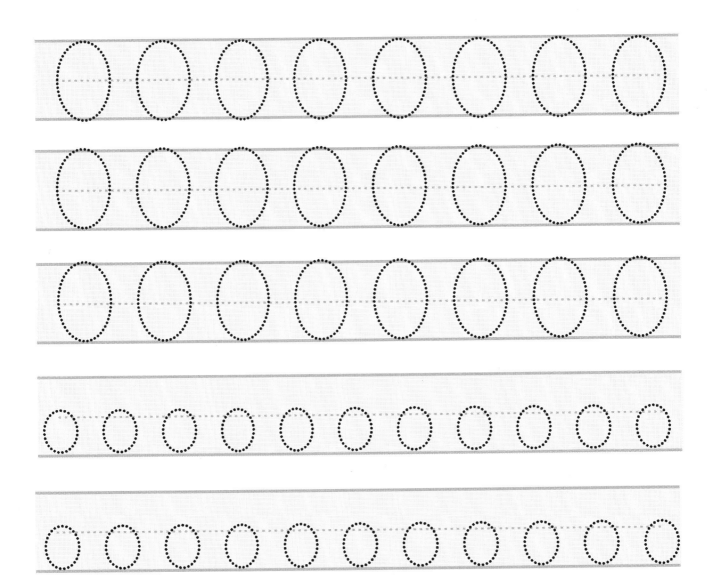

O

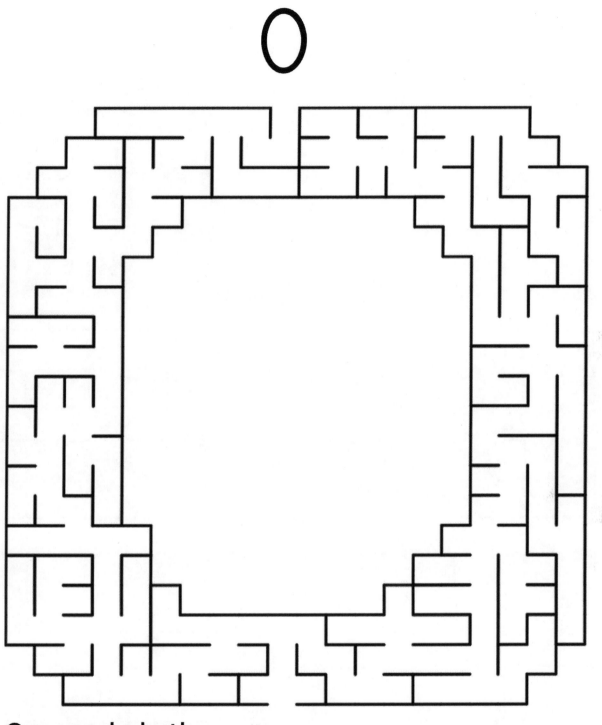

Can you help the
Owl find the O ?

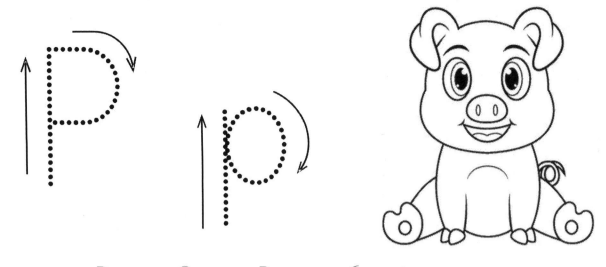

P is for Pig. Color me in

P is for Pig

P P P P P P P P P

P P P P P P P P P

P P P P P P P P P

p p p p p p p p p

p p p p p p p p p

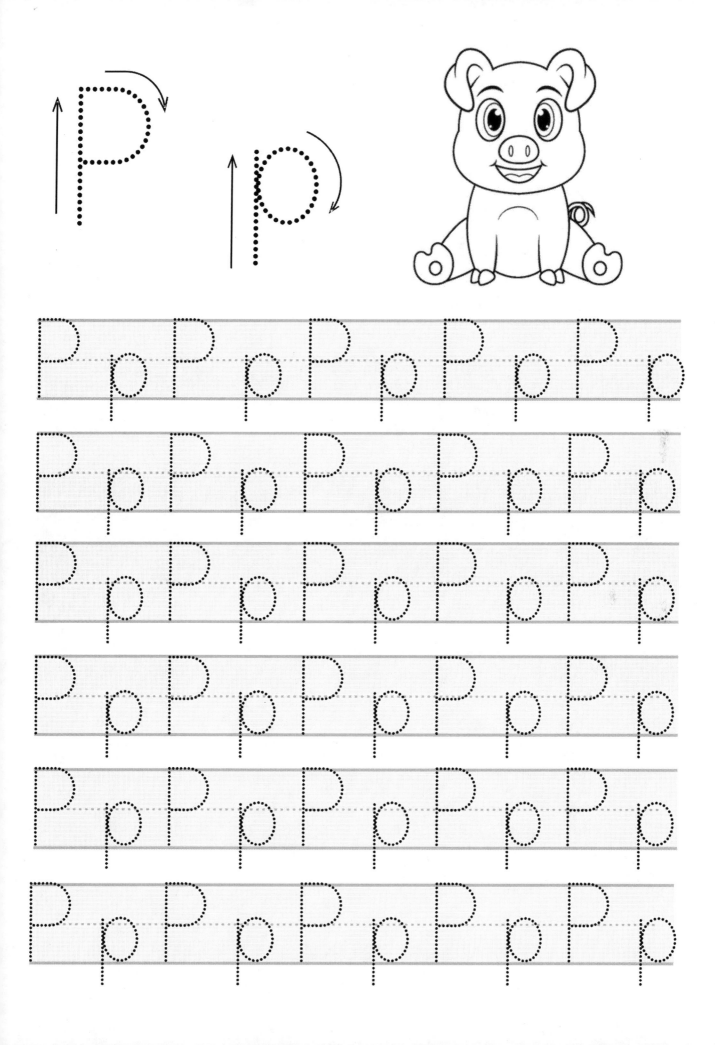

P

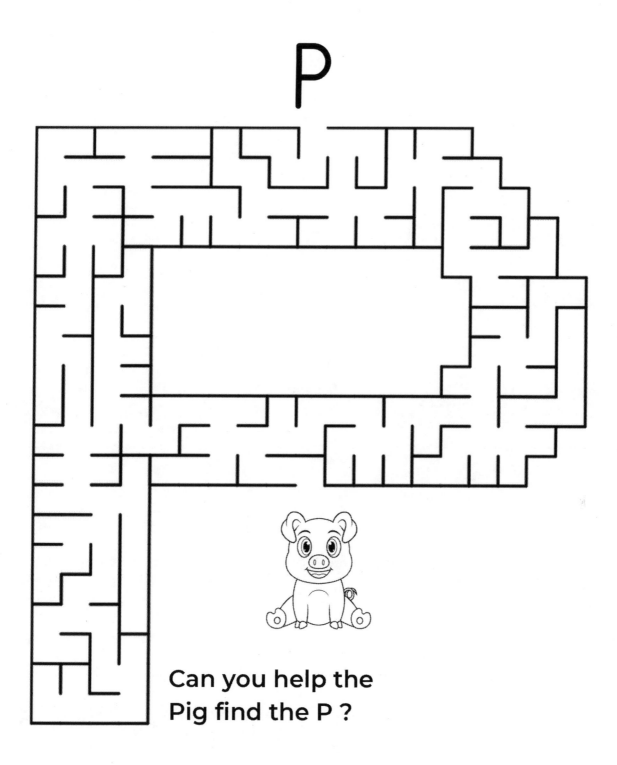

Can you help the
Pig find the P ?

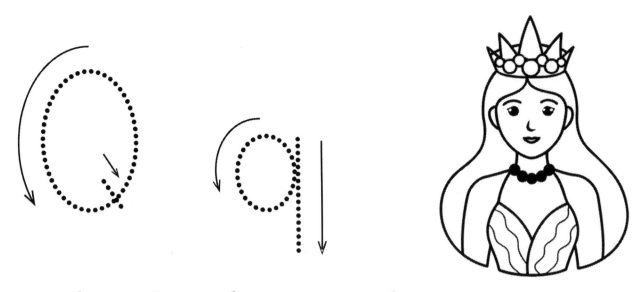

Q is for Queen. Color me in

Q is for Queen

Q Q Q Q Q Q Q

Q Q Q Q Q Q Q

Q Q Q Q Q Q Q

q q q q q q q q q q q q

q q q q q q q q q q q q

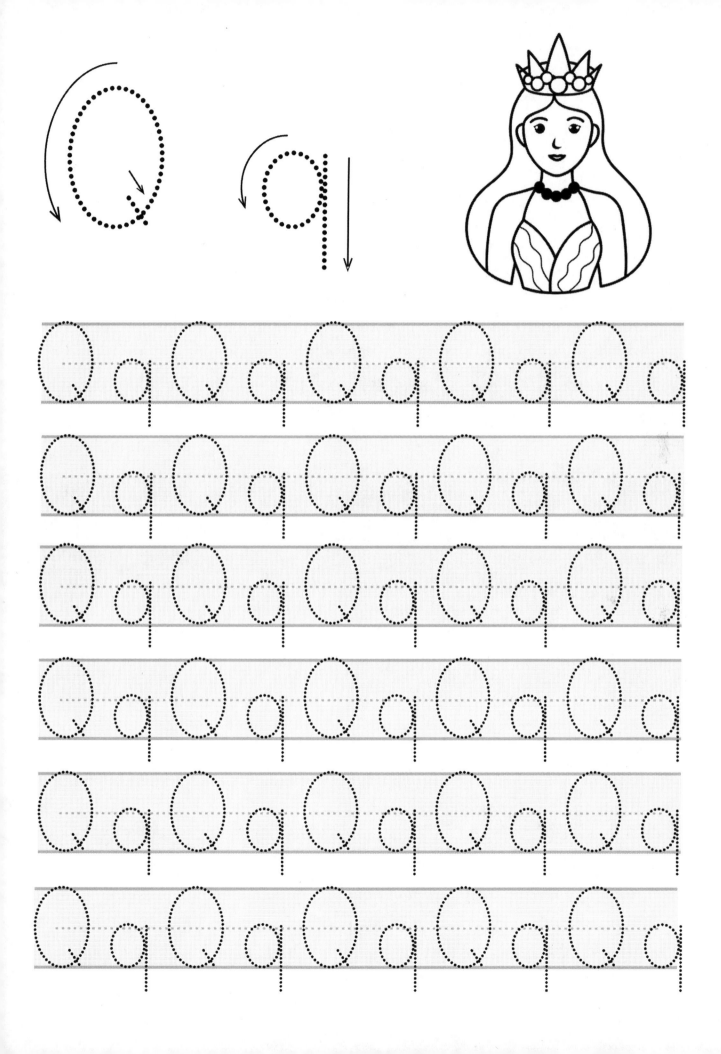

Q

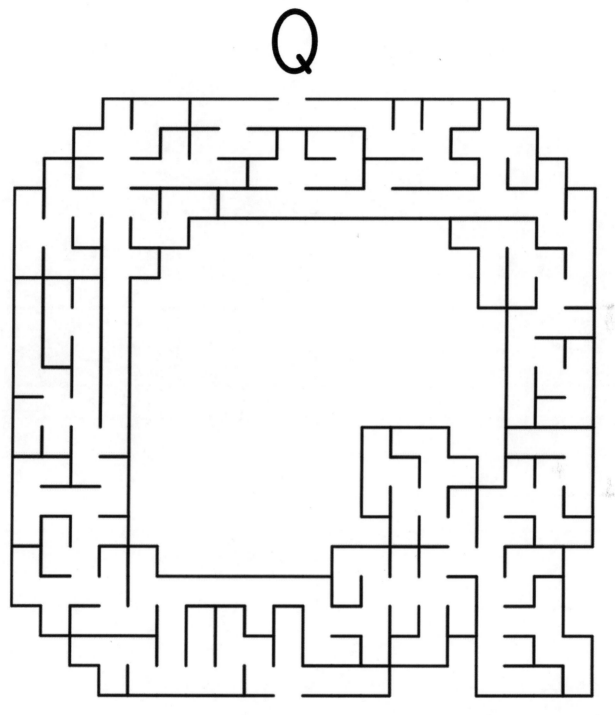

Can you help the
Queen find the Q ?

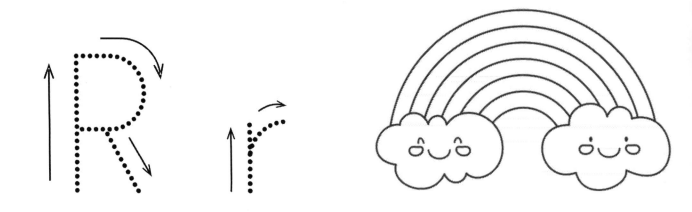

R is for Rainbow . Color me in

R is for Rainbow

R R R R R R R R R R

R R R R R R R R R R

R R R R R R R R R R

r r r r r r r r r r r

r r r r r r r r r r r r r r r r

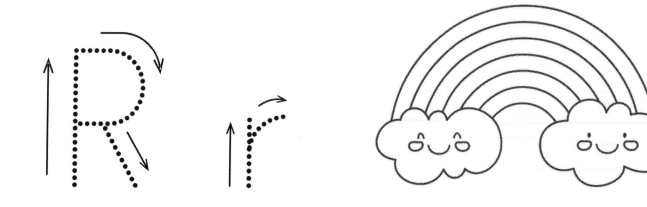

R r R r R r R r R r R r R r R r

R r R r R r R r R r R r R r R r

R r R r R r R r R r R r R r R r

R r R r R r R r R r R r R r R r

R r R r R r R r R r R r R r R r

R r R r R r R r R r R r R r R r

R

Can you help the
R find the Rainbow ?

S is for Strawberry. Color me in

S is for Strawberry

S

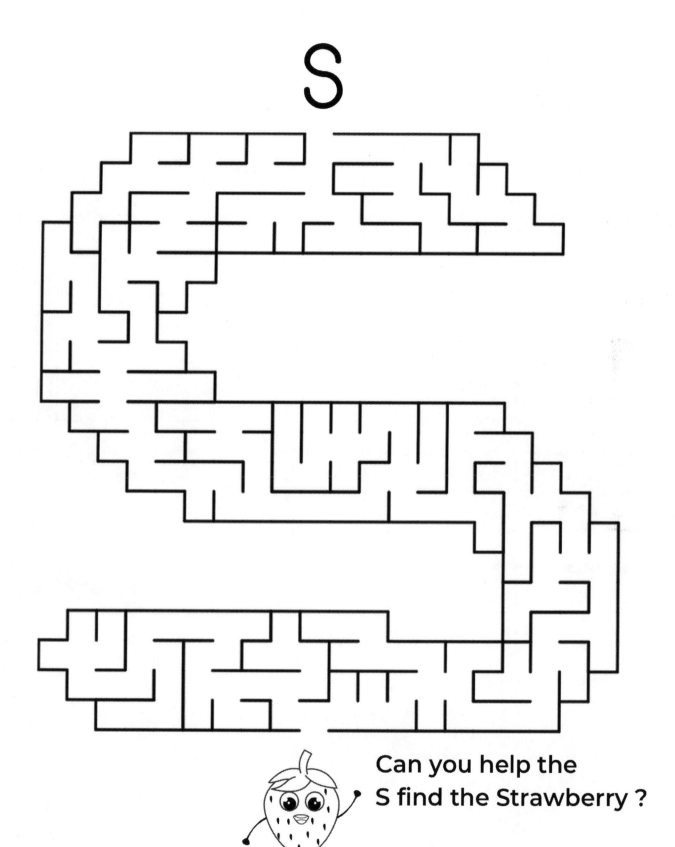

Can you help the
S find the Strawberry ?

T is for Train. Color me in

T is for Train

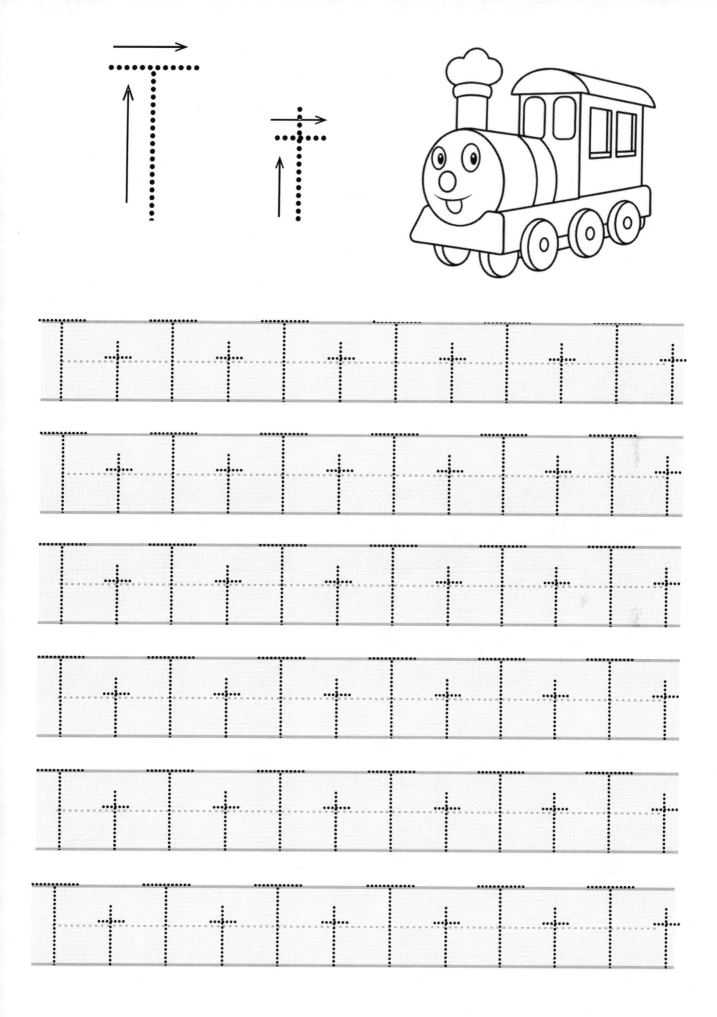

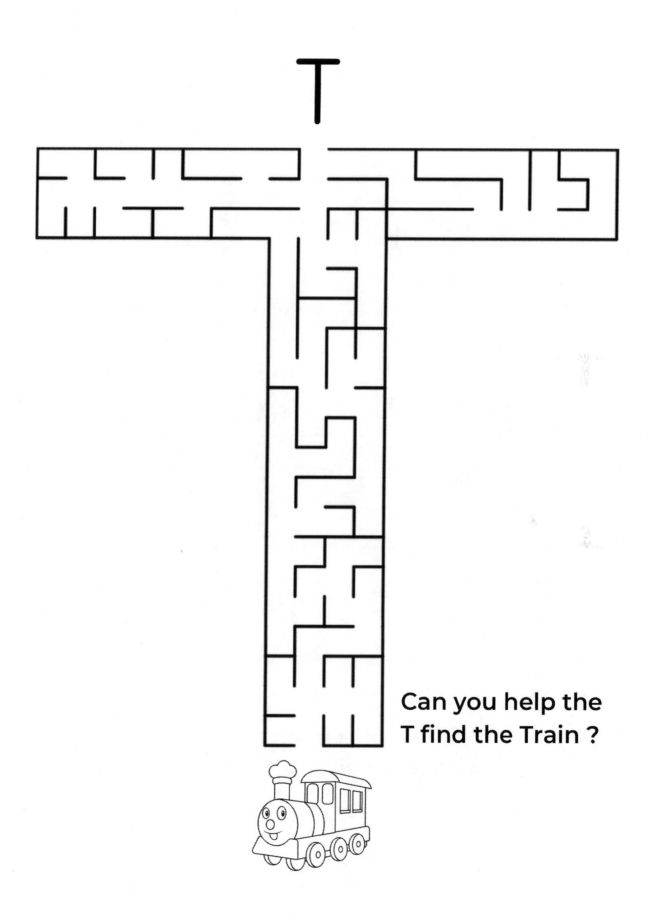

Can you help the
T find the Train ?

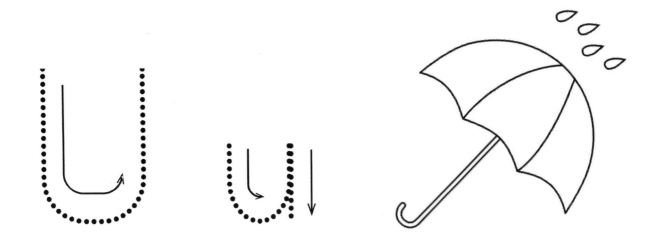

U is for Umbrella. Color me in

U is for Umbrella

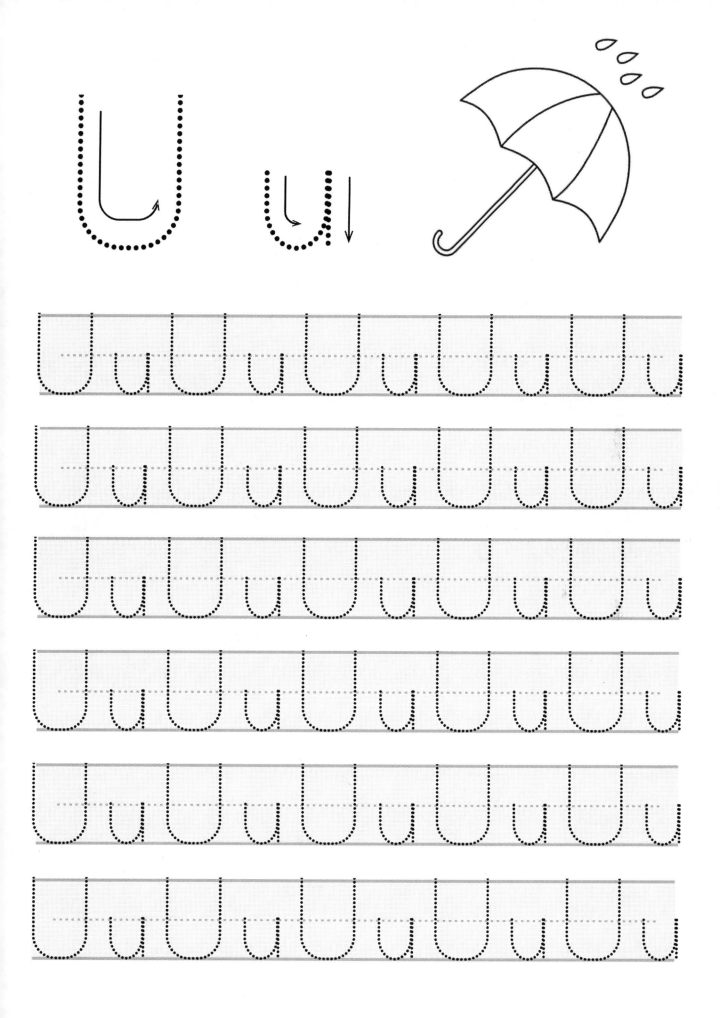

U

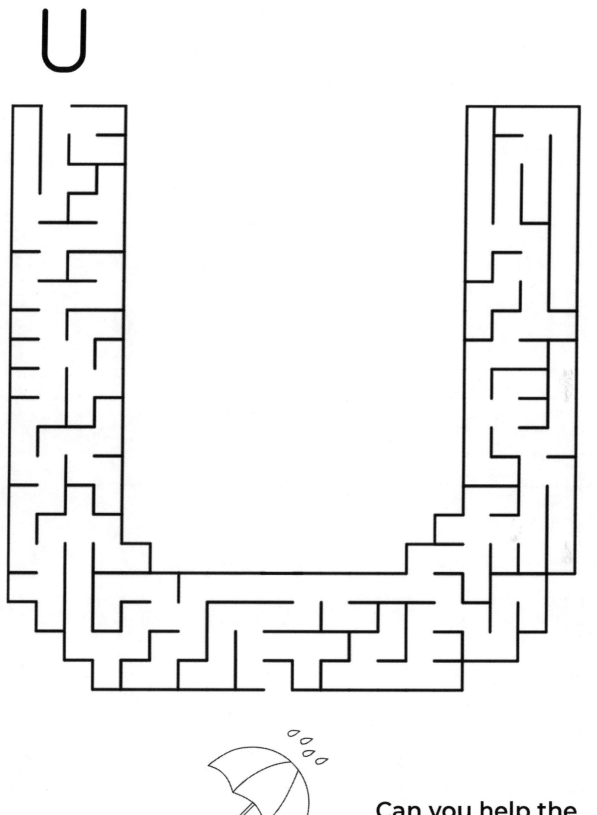

Can you help the
U find the Umbrella ?

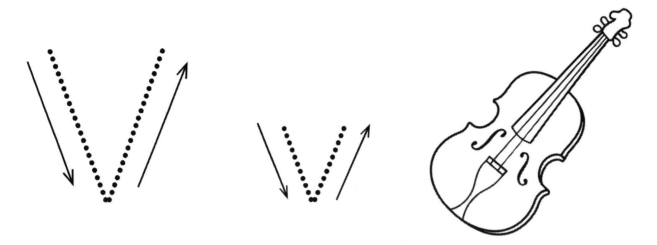

V is for Violin. Color me in

V is for Violin

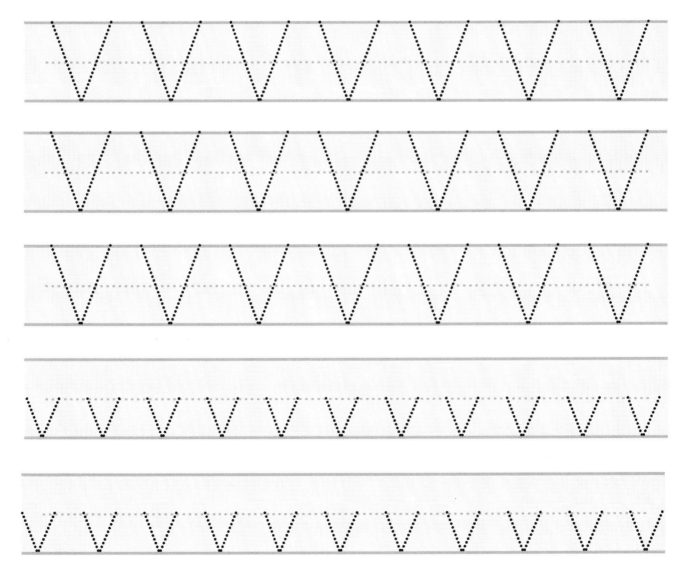

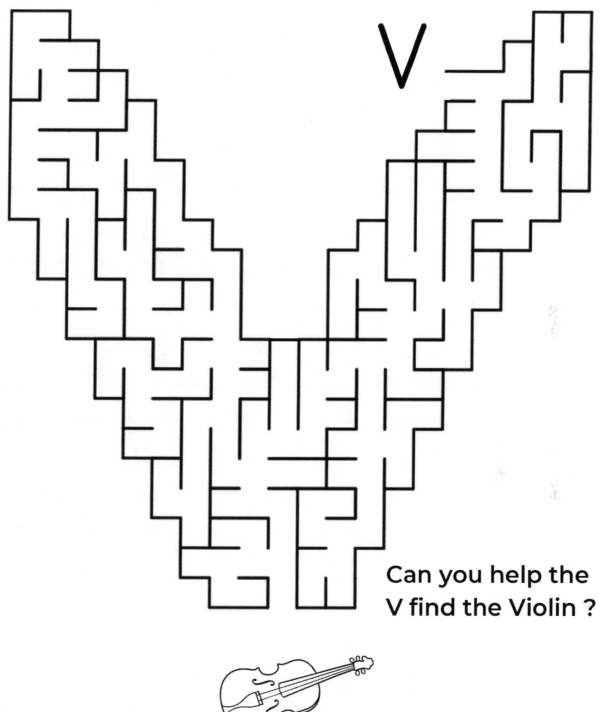

V

Can you help the
V find the Violin ?

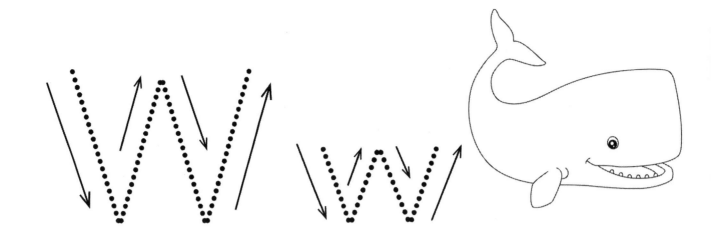

W is for Whale. Color me in

W is for Whale

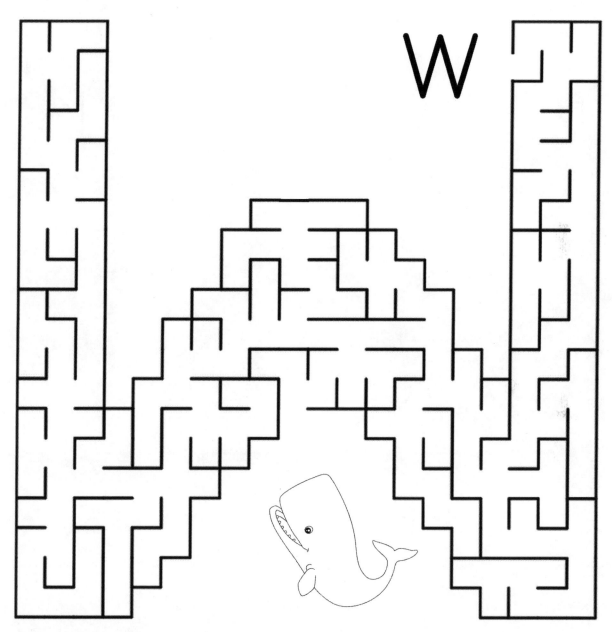

W

Can you help the
Whale find the W ?

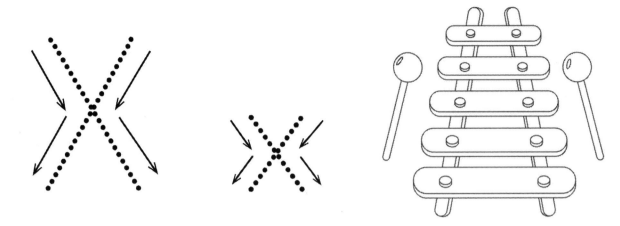

X is for Xylophone. Color me in

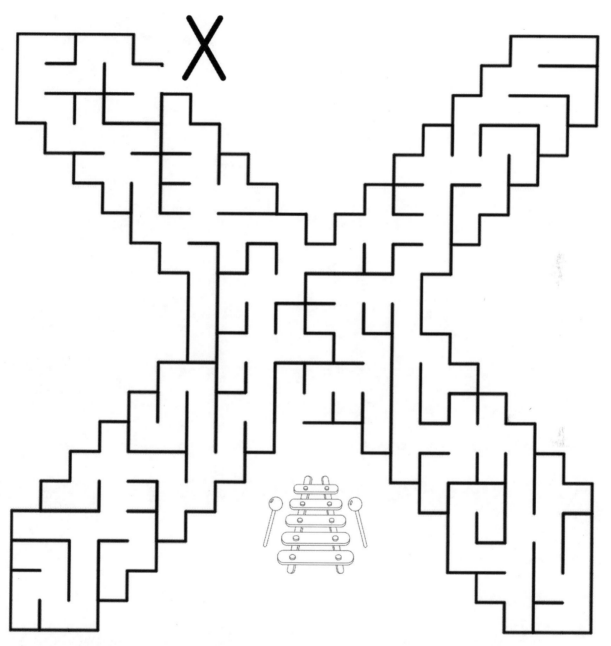

Can you help the X
find the Xylophone ?

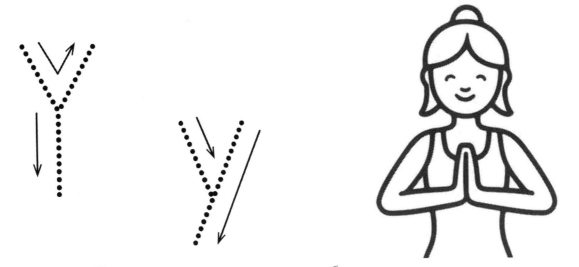

Y is for Yoga. Color me in

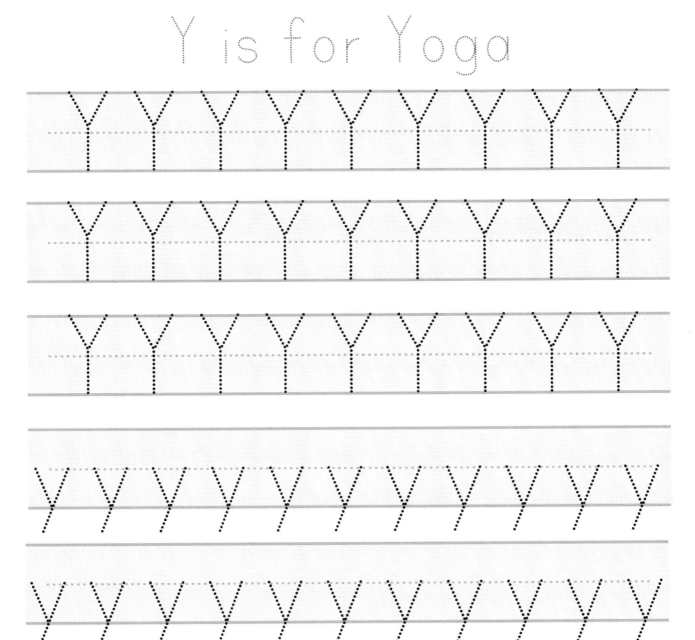

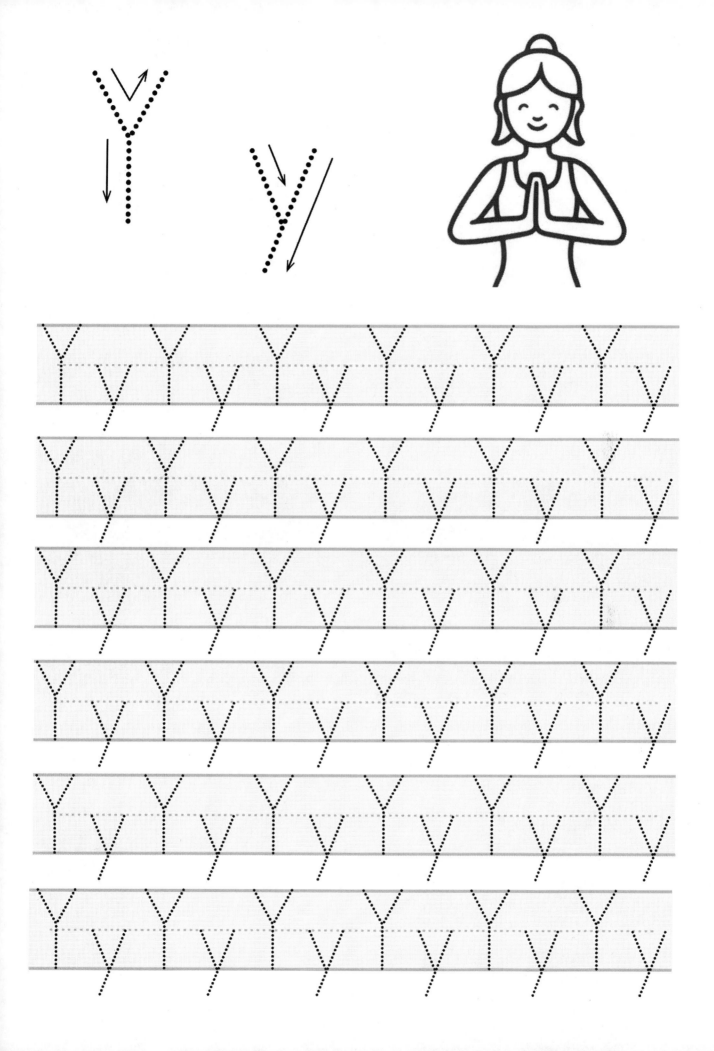

Can you help the Yoga teacher find the Y ?

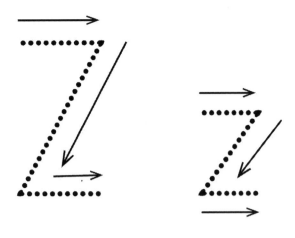 

Z is for Zebra. Color me in

Z is for Zebra

Z

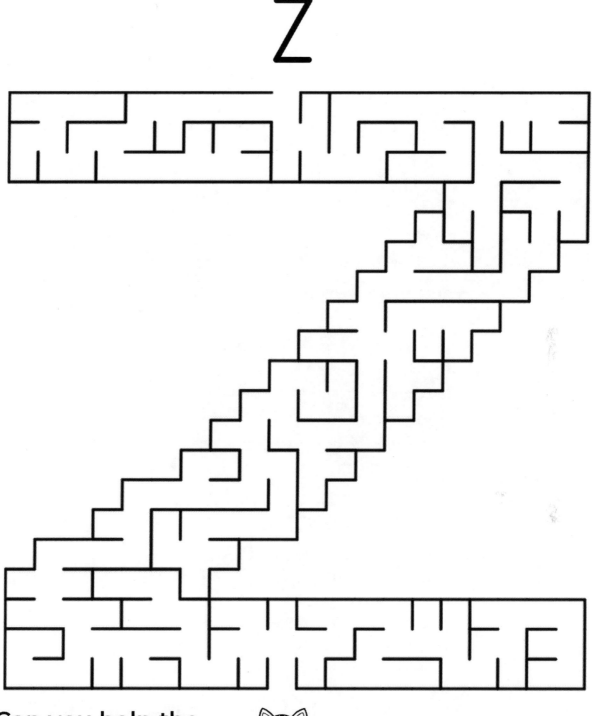

Can you help the
Zebra find the Z ?

CONGRATULATIONS!
You have reached the end of
your Letter Tracing Workbook.

You can continue to perfect
this life long skill as you grow
and learn. We wish you every
success that life has to offer.

Keep Writing!

Please consider leaving us a review on Amazon.
It only takes a few seconds to scan the code below
and leave a review. It really helps small publishers
like us. We greatly appreciate your support.

Thank you

Check out our other book!
Number Tracing for Kids ages 3-5

THANK YOU!

Made in the USA
Columbia, SC
19 November 2024

47097787R00061